CLIMB HIGH
CLIMB FAR
YOUR GOAL
THE SKY
YOUR AIM
THE STAR

WILLIAMS COLLEGE

Professor Rachel Rue's philosophy class in Griffin Hall

WILLIAMS
AT TWO HUNDRED

PHOTOGRAPHED BY BOB KRIST

Harmony House
Publishers~Louisville

Rare books in Chapin Library

Executive Editors: William Butler and William Strode
Library of Congress Catalog Number: 91-70932
Hardcover International Standard Book Number 0-916509-94-X
Printed in Canada by Friesen Printers, Manitoba, through
Four Colour Imports, Louisville
First Edition printed Fall, 1992 by Harmony House Publishers,
P.O. Box 90, Prospect, Kentucky 40059 (502) 228-2010/228-4446
Copyright © 1992 by Harmony House Publishers
Photographs copyright © 1992 by Robert Krist
Additional photography: Michael Lothner, pages 24-25,
Nicholas Whitman, page 73, Dennis Connors, pages 90-91.

Professor Deborah Bergstrand with student in Stetson Hall

Chapin Hall at twilight

PREFACE

After a visit to Williamstown in 1844, Henry David Thoreau observed that "it would be no small advantage if every college were thus located at the base of a mountain." Visitors ever since Thoreau have continued to think that Williams College is supremely fortunate in its mountain setting, with the Taconic Range to the west, Pine Cobble and the Dome to the north, and Greylock and its fellow monarchs dominating the skyline to the east. As the traveler nears Williamstown — and to my mind the approach up the ridge from Five Corners is the most beautiful — the views can literally take your breath away. In the valleys carved out by three rivers — the Hoosic, the Green, and Hemlock Brook — the New England village and the country college grew up together, and even today it is hard to say where campus ends and town begins.

Williams at 200 is the first of several books sponsored by the Williams College Bicentennial Commission to celebrate the 200th anniversary of the founding of this college in 1793. It is designed to capture Williams and Williamstown as they look today, in more than 100 stunning new color photographs never before printed.

Many of the scenes depicted in this book will be familiar to those who have long known the college and the town. Others will seem startlingly new — a hill and valley framed by buildings constructed or renovated in recent years, a campus landmark seen from a fresh angle, a revelatory human moment caught by the trained eye of a world-class photographer. Still others may stir memories of visits five or fifty years ago.

Photographer Bob Krist spent two cycles of the seasons in Williamstown taking some 10,000 color shots under the guidance of Craig Lewis '41, chairman of the Bicentennial Commission's Publications Committee, and fellow committee member Kristin Rehder, the college's director of development communications. From those 10,000, Pulitzer prize-winning photo editor Bill Strode (with the help of Lewis and Rehder) selected those that most vividly portray the Williams of today.

Although *Williams at 200* focuses on the present, the photographs in this book enable us to read the living history of the college. Some of the buildings — West College and Griffin Hall for example — date from the college's early years. Gray-stoned Morgan, foursquare Hopkins Hall (though updated), the old Lasell Gym with its clock, and the three Thompson science labs still wear the look of the late 19th century. Recent additions — the renovated College Museum of Art, the Chandler Athletic Center, and the Jewish Religious Center — reflect recent styles and commitments.

But the college is more than a collection of handsome red brick, gray stone, and white frame buildings; it is a community that joins its members in a common purpose and reaches across time. The people in these pictures represent the latest generation of the Williams family, but in a sense they walk in the footsteps of the thousands before them who spent time on this campus. Today's students and faculty carry on old traditions and invent new rituals. Those who contemplate these photographs, whether or not they have recently revisited Williamstown, can still inhabit the dwelling of "the gallant and the free."

Dustin H. Griffin II '65
Chairman, Bicentennial Commission

Reunion classes gathering

INTRODUCTION

By John M. Hyde '52
Professor of History

As institutions and individuals age, they are honored for their longevity at auspicious intervals of time — decades for individuals, centuries for institutions. Founded in 1793, Williams College is approaching such a milestone in its history, thereby joining that select few of American colleges and universities which, like the nation itself, have celebrated their bicentennial. In an era which disdains historical names and dates, it is worth noting that George Washington was President of the United States when Williams College came into being. To mark the occasion, this entirely new portfolio of Williams photographs is being published.

What the camera records is only a moment in the history of the college. Those of us who are alumni have shared other moments in that history, moments which include not only our own experiences as undergraduates but the experiences of others as told to us by our parents, friends, and children or as captured in old photographs, letters, and diaries. Together they make up what the historian Carl Becker called our "specious present," an awareness of the present that is enlarged and enriched by what we remember and what others have written or told us they remember. We thereby become our own historians who, as we look through these photographs, bring to them our own histories, recognizing the

people and places that are familiar, that recall our own experiences, and at the same time noting the changes that have taken place. Each history will differ, reminding us that the college, just as the society it serves, is always in a state of transition.

My "specious present" reaches back to the Reverend Alvan Hyde who became a Williams trustee in 1802. He was also serving as Vice President of Williams in 1821 when a significant number of the undergraduates followed President Zephaniah Swift Moore over the mountains to found Amherst — allegedly accompanied by books from the Williams library. The trustees delegated to the "venerable" Doctor Hyde the daunting responsibility of persuading the small, beleaguered "rump" of undergraduates who had not defected with President Moore to remain in Williamstown and to assure them of the trustees' continued support for the college. Alvan's son Alexander, of the Class of 1834, was sent over the mountains to obtain from Union College a charter for a Phi Beta Kappa chapter. Failing in that endeavor, he returned with a Kappa Alpha key, thereby introducing the forerunner of national fraternities onto the Williams campus.

Earliest memories in my own case are of the college on the eve of the Second World War, watching an ice hockey game on the "rink" below the Cole Field House and observing the graduation exercises of the Class of 1941, which included a cousin who was to meet death in the skies over Holland two years later. Since that time, I have observed, participated in, and in a small measure helped to direct the affairs of this college as student, alumnus, professor, and dean. For me, therefore, these photographs are very much a part of my "specious present."

The most dramatic change over the past half-century has been the increase in the size and diversity not only of the student body, but of the faculty, staff, and administration as well. This diversity of gender, race, ethnicity, religion, of geographical and socio-economic backgrounds, is revealed in the photographs of activities and events that mark the college year. Be forewarned, however, that these are the most transitory of all the subjects in this photographic record. The life of a residential college moves quickly from one moment to the next. Preferences in dress, language, music, and food, the relative strengths of athletic teams, the objects and forms of protest, the popularity of certain courses and majors—all are in constant flux. What one college generation defines as "signficant" or "fun" becomes, in turn, irrelevant and boring to the next. A "tradition" for undergraduates becomes something that began before they came to college. "Traditions," like the college itself, are always in transition. The photographer can only capture the moment. Even before the picture is published, it may have become a historical document.

Curricular change does not lend itself to photography, but it inevitably reflects the explosion of knowledge and the awareness of the world beyond the West that have manifested themselves in our world. Let us not be too arrogant, however, about our role in bringing about these changes. The Haystack Monument is a symbol of that wide-world awareness among the earliest Williams undergraduates, young men who, as Hawthorne noted, were "unpolished bumpkins" from the surrounding farms and small towns of New England.

In carrying out these curricular changes, the college has remained true to that image which above all others has been associated with Williams—that of Mark Hopkins on one end of the log and a student on the other. Williams continues to devote its energies and resources to the education of undergraduates on a scale that not only allows but demands a direct, personal contact between student and faculty. In this endeavor, the "log" has taken many forms over the years. You will recognize many of the classrooms in these photographs — including the campus lawns — while others will be new or transformed spaces. The classroom remains the heart of the enterprise, for it is there that the exchange between student and faculty must take place. Each individual will be able to name a favorite successor to Mark Hopkins on the other end of

West College and Clark Hall

the log. The faces in the classroom will change; the content of the courses will vary; but the log remains in place. Education at Williams has retained its human scale.

What photographs reveal most effectively is the setting of the college — the buildings, the natural surroundings, the seasons of the year. The Williams campus was never dominated by one style of architecture that succeeding generations felt compelled to emulate. Instead, it became a diverse collection of buildings that, for good or ill, reflected the changing styles and tastes of American architecture — from the Georgian simplicity of West and Griffin to the "disconnected" pillars at the south end of the modern addition to Lawrence Hall. But it is the natural setting with which the college has been most closely identified.

In their petition to the Massachusetts Legislature, the founders of the college defended their choice of a location for the proposed academy as being in "an enclosed place," far removed from the "temptations and allurements" of seaport towns. At official functions, we sing our praises of the mountains and of "grand old Greylock's lofty wooded crown." One of the coaches interrupts practices on Cole Field with "time out for beauty," urging his charges to revel in the glory of autumn and of the mountains. For nearly 200 years, Williams students have lived and learned "'neath the shadow of the hills." For some, it is true, they represent isolation and separation from a more vibrant world. For most, however, the mountains are a comforting and reassuring presence that greet them daily in their lives as undergraduates and upon their return as alumni. They are an inherent part of the experience and memory of all who have passed through this valley.

This photographic record of Williams College is a celebration of the college's bicentennial and of the photographer's art. It is an interpretation of the contemporary scene that will appeal to those who have known the college personally or have only learned about it from others. Each of us, in turn, will interpret these photographs in the light of our own experiences — the names and faces, the jokes and stories, the songs and sounds they bring to mind. As members of the "academy," past and present, we share a common sense of place and purpose, a moment in each of our lives when we began to be aware of ourselves as individuals separate from our parents, to try out ideas, to make our own mistakes, to define — tentatively at best — the ideals and values by which we hoped to live. May this collection recall, therefore, the sense of place, this "mountain land," but also the sense of purpose for which Williams College was established two centuries ago and of which we have been the beneficiaries.

Environmental field trip on the Hoosic River

Overleaf: Professor Raymond Chang teaching chemistry

lectrons repel one

$= pK_a + \log \dfrac{[\text{conjugate base}]}{[\text{Ea}]}$

Weak ac

protein

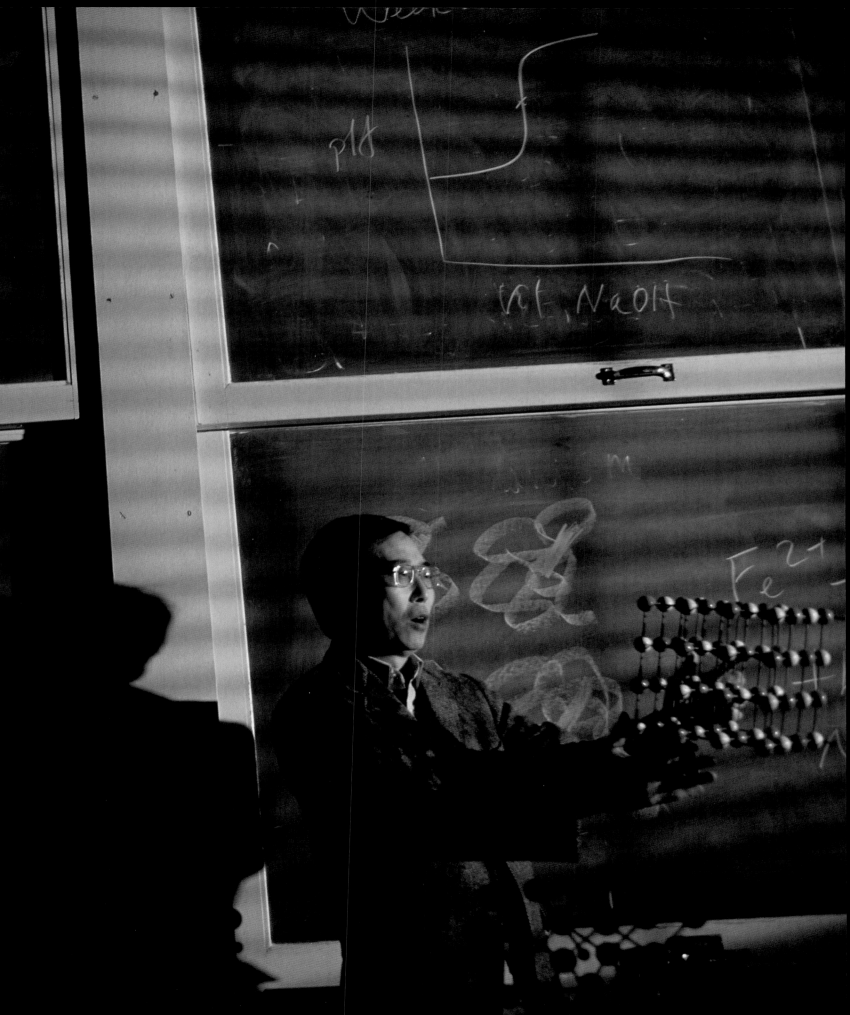

WILLIAMS : A SELECTIVE CHRONOLOGY

1755　Col. Ephraim Williams is killed in battle seven weeks after signing a will conditionally funding a free school in the township west of Fort Massachusetts.

1765　The township is renamed Williamstown, fulfilling one of the will's conditions.

1787　Williamstown is confirmed to be within Massachusetts — another Eph condition.

1791　Free school opens with Ebenezer Fitch as preceptor in what is now West College.

1792　Trustees petition for college status seven months after the school's opening.

1793　Massachusetts Legislature approves the petition. Williams College opens October 9th with 18 students and Fitch as president.

1806　Haystack prayer meeting inspires five Williams students to launch the U.S. foreign missions movement.

1815　Fitch resigns saying the College has no future in Williamstown: "no way to save it from extinction but to remove it."

1819　His successor Zephaniah Swift Moore petitions for permission to relocate the College in Northampton.

1820　No! Relocation would be "neither lawful nor expedient," the Massachusetts Legislature replies.

1821　Moore resigns to preside over the Collegiate Institution at Amherst. Many students leave with him. Seeing Williams foundering, graduates organize the world's first Society

1828　Griffin Hall caps the College's comeback under President Edward Dorr Griffin, making it a three-building campus with more than 100 students enrolled from 1830 on.

1836　Mark Hopkins begins a 36-year presidency that puts new emphasis on inspired teaching — and puts Williams on the map.

1838　Hopkins Observatory opens, brother Albert's creation, the first in the U.S. built exclusively for that purpose.

1859　The country's first intercollegiate baseball game: Williams 32, Amherst 73.

1871　Future U.S. President James A. Garfield wraps up the Hopkins era with legendary words: "The ideal college is Mark Hopkins on one end of a log and a student on the other."

1882　Morgan Hall is the first of six landmark buildings completed under Franklin Carter in time for the College's Centennial: Morgan, Hopkins, Lasell, three Thompson labs.

1889　Graduation of Gaius Bolin, first black student at Williams.

1900　Turn-of-the-century enrollments climb toward 400.

1921　President Harry Garfield's Institute of Politics brings world notables to Williamstown for 12 straight summers, making the College internationally known.

1923　Williams gets a library within a library — the priceless Chapin collection of rare books in

1927   Williams enrollments surpass 800 this year and for five straight years until the Depression hits.

1934   New President Tyler Dennett mounts a frontal assault on student loafing, fraternity excesses, faculty deadwood. Most dramatic result: 45% faculty turnover in three years.

1937   Dennett challenges the College's admission policies ("too many nice boys") and property purchases (Greylock corner). Widening differences with Williams trustees bring on his abrupt resignation at midyear.

1941   President James Phinney Baxter is tapped for Washington service four months before Pearl Harbor. The wartime campus is taken over by Navy trainees. Williams students dwindle to a graduating class of four in June 1945.

1946   The great postwar comeback brings peak enrollment: 1,060 Williams students, 778 of them veterans, 69 with wives.

1951   Sterling Committee faults fraternities for having "magnified social inequality." College cracks down on restrictive clauses, bars freshmen from membership, builds Baxter Hall as their dining and social center in 1953.

1962   Fraternity review committee appointed by President John Sawyer — the Angevine Committee — recommends that the College take over fraternity functions.

1965   Greylock Quad sets the pattern for small-group living without fraternities — four residential houses with their own dining hall

1968   Bronfman Science Center opens. Fraternities are asked to terminate all activities at Williams.

1969   Lockwood Committee recommends enrolling women and enlarging the College to accommodate them. The first waves arrive.

1975   First four-year women receive B.A.s from President John Chandler. Williams enrollments rise above 1,800. The Sawyer Library is dedicated.

1979   Bernhard Music Center adds new heft to the arts at Williams, as do subsequent additions to the College's art museum and theatre in 1983.

1983   New Alumni Center opens on Main Street.

1984   Four-building campus at Oxford acquired for Williams students spending a study-abroad year there.

1987   Chandler Athletic Center dedicated by the President Emeritus and his successor Francis Oakley.

1989   Bolin Centennial brings many of the College's 550 black graduates back to celebrate.

1990   Jewish Religious Center dedicated to meet a College and community need.

1991   The winningest Williams football team stretches its streak to 23 games before Trinity snaps it on a last-second play.

1993   Bicentennial celebrations begin with multiple Eph's Birthday parties March 6th and climax with Convocation Weekend on October 9th, the College's 200th birthday.

One of the considerable strengths of this college with its human scale and community spirit is that students and teachers may easily step out of their respective professional roles and relate to one another simply as human beings... Then the larger perplexities and questions that are on the minds of students, and often on the minds of their teachers as well, will find a natural forum that augments the function of the classroom.

President John W. Chandler in his induction address, 1973

Professor Henry Art conferring with pre-med student

Preceding page: Outdoor class seen from Hopkins Hall's north entrance

Afternoon break in Currier Hall

Hopkins Gate, West College

Science Quad seen from chapel tower

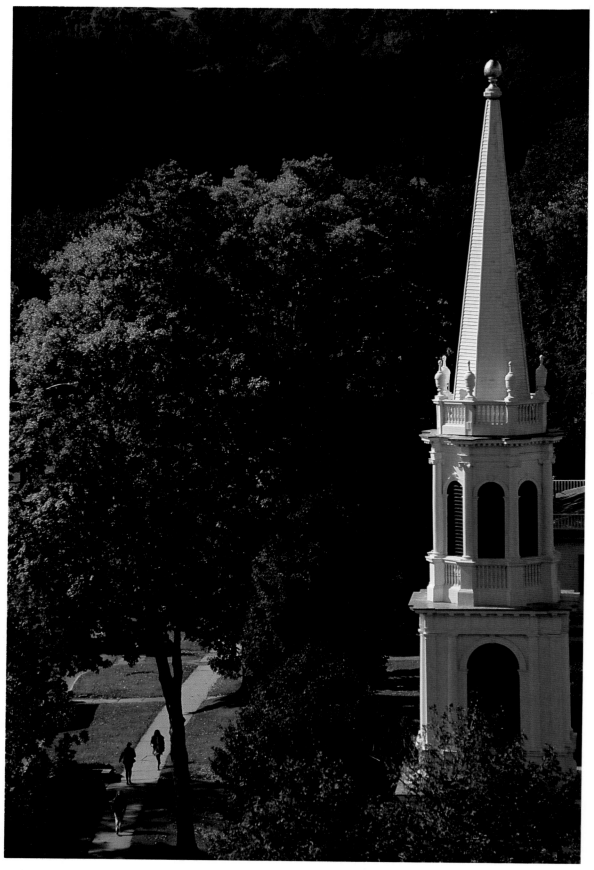

Congregational church spire

Civil War monument, Griffin Hall

Jewish Religious Center

Overleaf: Self-correcting sundial on Science Quad

39

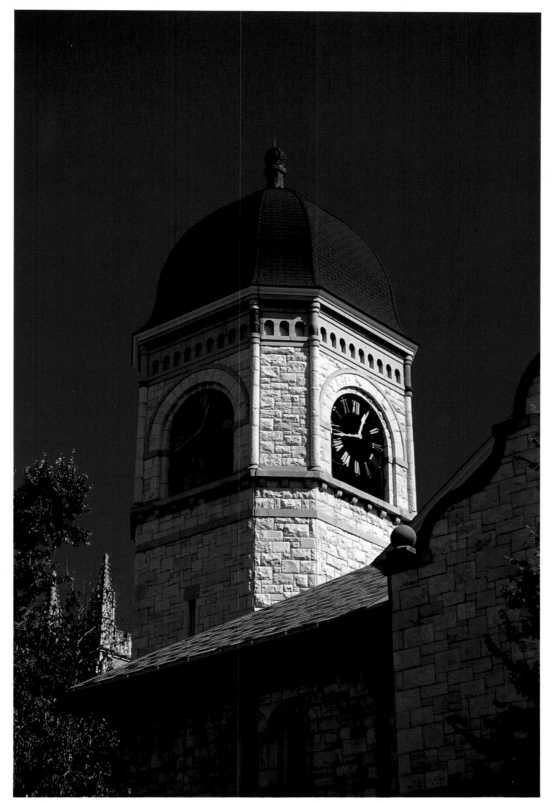

Lasell Gym clock tower

View from inside Lasell Gym clock

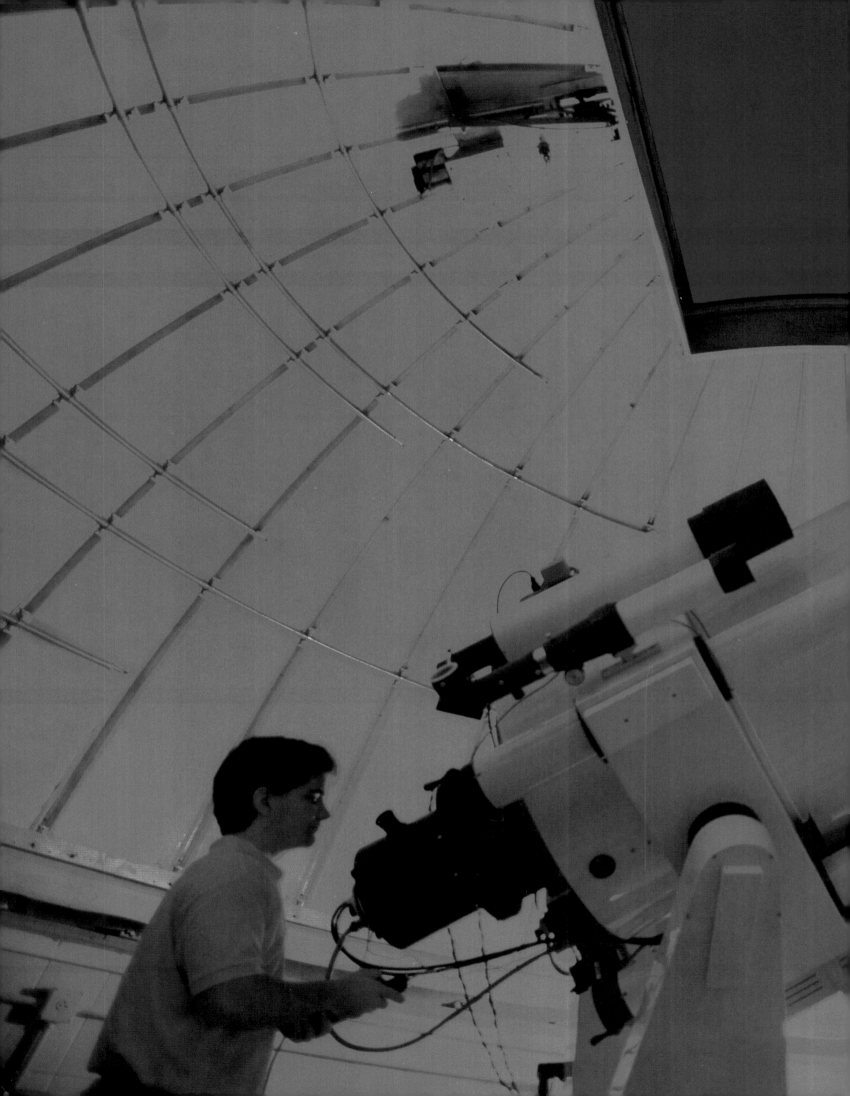

Mapping the stars with reflector telescope atop physics building   45

Student in computer lab, Jesup Hall

We are to regard the mind not as a piece of iron to be laid upon the anvil and hammered into any shape, nor as a block of marble in which we are to find the statue by removing the rubbish, nor as a receptacle into which knowledge may be poured; but as a flame that is to be fed, as an active being that must be strengthened to think and to feel — to dare, to do, and to suffer.

President Mark Hopkins, Williams 1824, in his induction address, 1836

Bronfman Science Center library

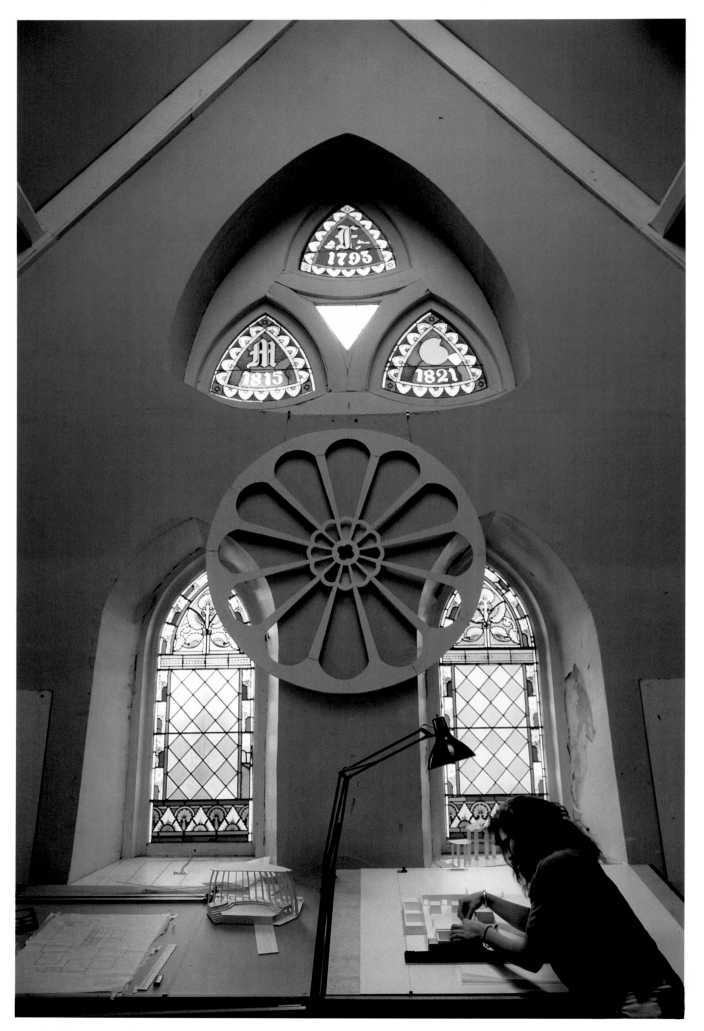

50   *Architecture studio in Goodrich Hall*

Professor Irwin Shainman's symphony course, Bernhard Music Center

51

I have always been struck by the sheer numbers of alumni who go out of their way to recall for me how in some important respect their lives have been touched by one or other member of the faculty. . . Who among our alumni does not harbor memories of their experiences with such fine teachers of past years as Vince Barnett, Lane Faison, Bob Gaudino, Don Gifford, Charlie Keller, Sam Matthews, Bill Miller, Dick Newhall, David Park, Bill Pierson, Don Richmond, Fred Rudolph, Fred Schuman, Bob Scott, and Whit Stoddard?

President Francis Oakley in his 1990 President's Report

Three professors at work—Charles Fuqua, David L. Smith, Whitney Stoddard

President Francis Oakley in Hopkins Hall office

Professor Fred Greene teaching political science, Hopkins Hall

54

Class-changing time on campus

My attachment to Williams is necessarily influenced by a romantic appreciation of its uniqueness... what might be called a spirit... best represented by such vignettes of Williams life as the marching band invading the barber shop during football season; or the kite-flying competition; or the female coxswain on a 166-year-long all-male crew.

Gair Hemphill Crutcher 1971, one of the first seven women to receive B.A.s from Williams

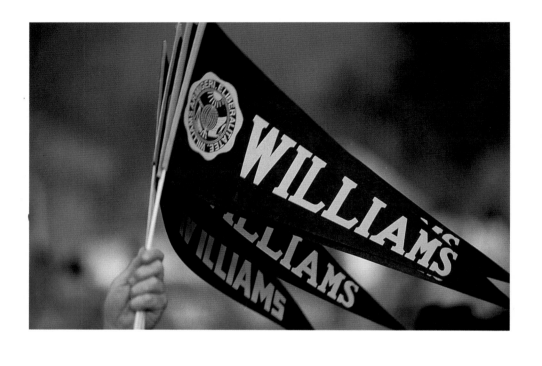

Tailgate parties at Weston Field

Football fans at Homecoming

Education is not a process that can wholly be confined to classroom, laboratory, studio, or library... The diverse experience and richly variegated moments of life in a residential community must all combine to make their particular contribution: extracurriculum as well as curriculum; play as well as work; fellowship as well as solitude; the foreign as well as the familiar; discomfort as well as ease; protest as well as celebration.

President Francis Oakley in his induction address, 1985

Christmas at Thompson Memorial Chapel

Preceding pages: Celebrating the second straight undefeated season

President's House

West College on a wintry afternoon

Rotunda, Williams College Museum of Art

Students perform with Berkshire Symphony, Chapin Hall

Williams-Oxford students at Exeter College, Oxford

74

Dining at Exeter College, Oxford

Canopy walkway in the college's Hopkins Forest

South Williamstown's Modern Dairy Farm

Valley view from the Hairpin Turn

Team photographs in Lasell Gym

Scenes at the Log

Spring Street shops

I shall never forget that evening when I first entered Williamstown, riding on the top of the North Adams stage. The September rains had been abundant, and the meadows and slopes were at their greenest; the atmosphere was as nearly transparent as we are apt to see; the sun was just sinking behind the Taconics, and the shadows were creeping up the eastern slopes of [Mounts] Williams and Prospect; the outlines of [Mount Greylock] were defined against a sky as rich and deep as ever looked down at sunset on Naples or Palermo. I thought then that I had never seen a lovelier valley.

Reverend Washington Gladden, Williams 1859, composer of *The Mountains*, writing in the *Williams Weekly*, October 1893

Morgan Hall

At home in Tyler House

There is an intensity to Williams that catches you by surprise. It's more than just academics. It's the entire experience, from the location itself and the friendships with other students to the value placed on participation and performance. My appreciation for the experience has grown a great deal in the ten years I have been away.

Lee F. Jackson 1979, Treasurer, City of Boston, in 1989

95

Teeing off at Taconic Golf Course

Diving practice, Chandler Athletic Center

Women's soccer practice, Cole Field

Hoopsters in Chandler Athletic Center

Class Day, Science Quad

Light Night, Baxter Hall

I wonder if all the puffery about Williams educating the leaders of the future is counter-productive. Someone smart enough to come here knows what the leaders of the future are up against. This society will reward your brains and sophistication, but only your character will impel you to the risks of leadership. If there is hope for us all, it lies in those risks and your willingness to run them.

Kai N. Lee, Professor of Environmental Studies, in 1992

Watch drop from the chapel tower

Commencement scenes

111

I have never forgotten that I am a Williams man, and… if there is any one thing in the world of which I am proud almost to foolishness, it is that fact.

Gaius Charles Bolin, Williams 1889, the College's first black graduate

Reunion scenes

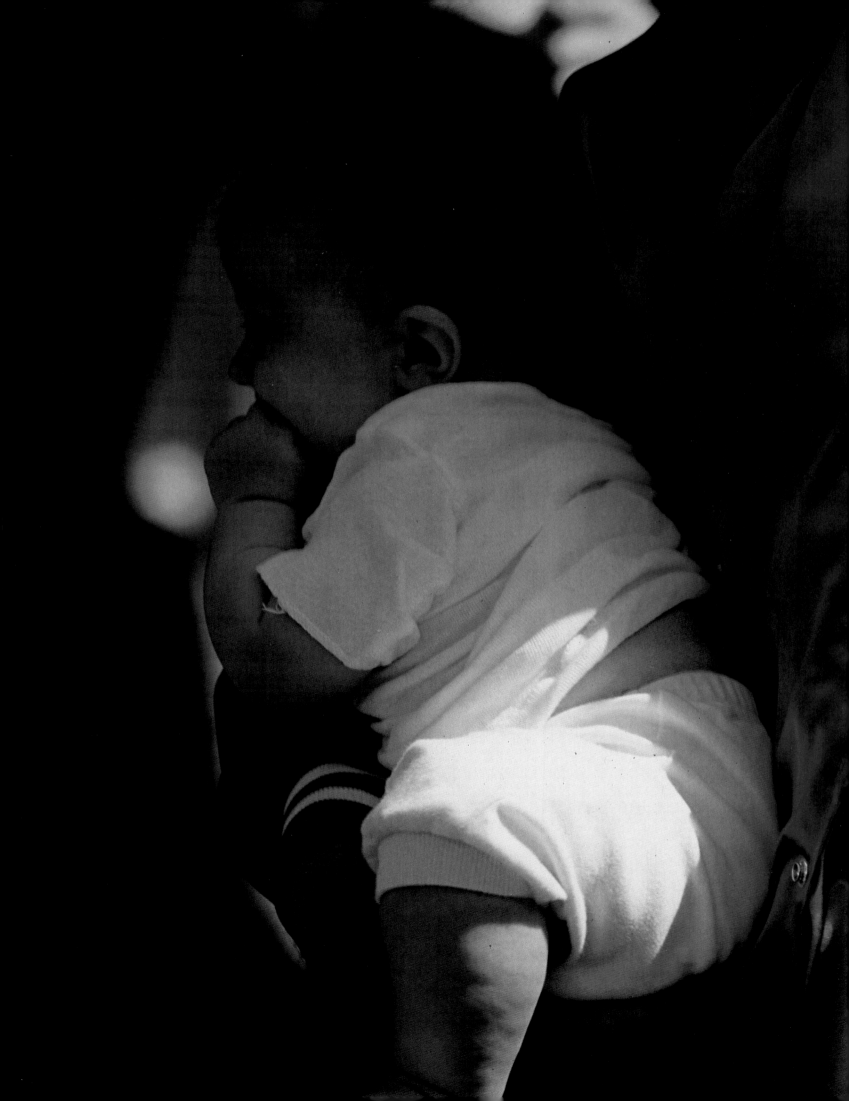

Reunion parade down Main Street

Kansas City alumni recently invited me to come there and give a talk. The way people responded after the talk — the incisive questions they asked — was impressive. Seeing what people do with their lives after they leave here reminds you of how rich they are as human beings and their potential while you're with them at Williams.

Zirka Z. Filipczak, the Massachusetts Professor of Art, in 1992

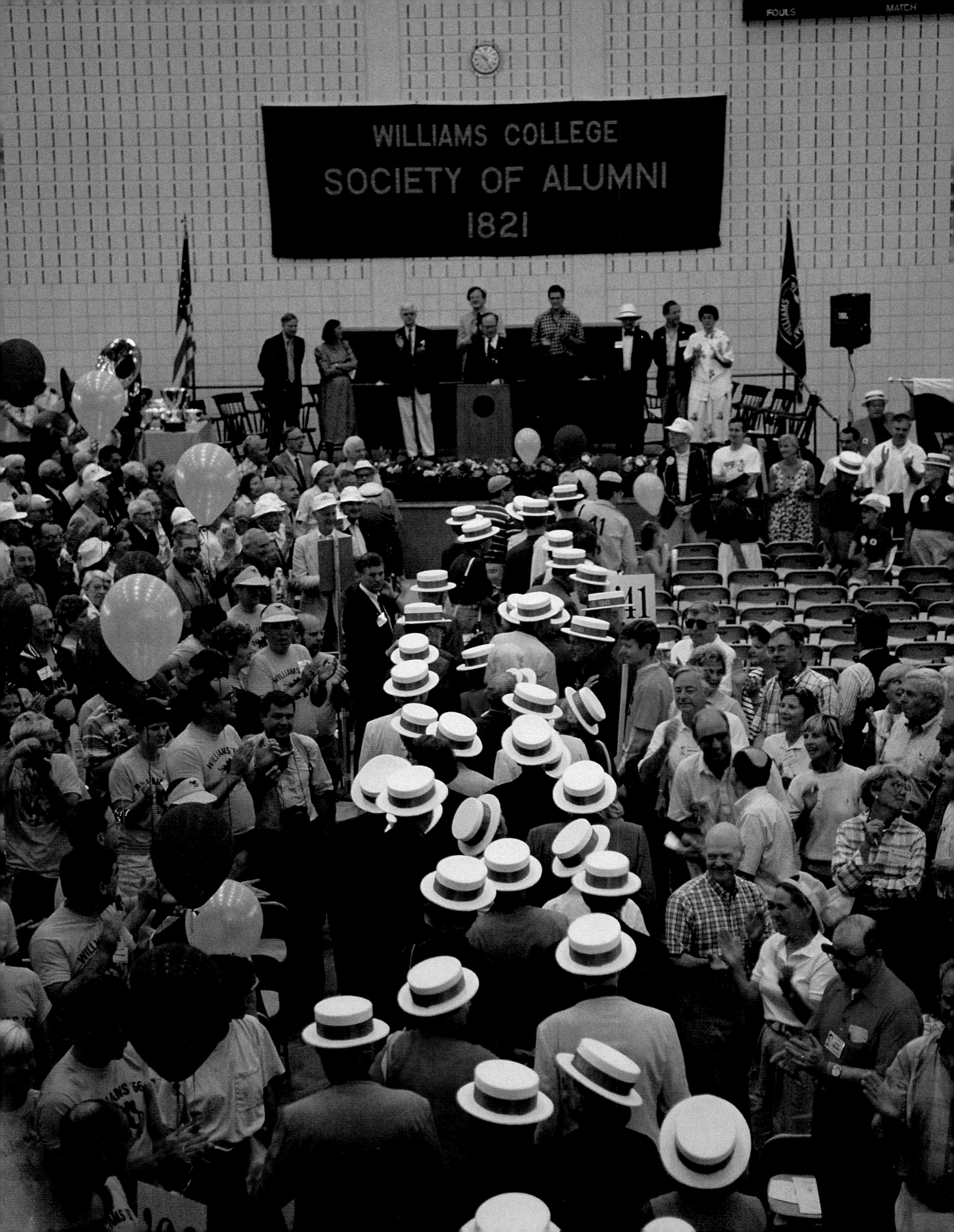
FOULS
MATCH
WILLIAMS COLLEGE
SOCIETY OF ALUMNI
1821
41

Memorial service, Thompson Chapel

Annual meeting, Society of Alumni

At Mount Hope